This book belongs to

_____

ANIMALS
AND THEIR BABIES

WALT DISNEY FUN-TO-LEARN LIBRARY

ISBN 0-9619525-6-3
Advance Publishers Inc., P.O. Box 2607, Winter Park, FL. 32790
Printed in the United States of America
0987654321

Mowgli was puzzled. He was beginning to notice that he was different from his wolf brothers and sisters.

"Of course you're different," said Mother Wolf when he asked her about it. "We're wolves. You're a man-cub."

"Then tell me about wolves, Mother," Mowgli said.

"Wolves and foxes and even pet dogs all belong to one big family," said Mother Wolf. "We are all dogs. We are the same in many ways. We are different in other ways...."

Wolves live together in families called packs. All the wolves in the pack help with the hunt, and help to feed and take care of the babies.

The little wolf cubs play like puppies. They watch the hunting games of the older wolves. And when they are old enough, they learn to hunt with the pack.

"Then there are jackals," said Mother Wolf. "You have heard jackals howling in the evening. . . ."

"They sound funny," said Mowgli.

"Sometimes jackals eat the leftovers of other animals," said Mother Wolf. "But sometimes they hunt at night and bring home food for their cubs.

"The smallest wolves are called coyotes. They are night hunters who sing to the moon."

"I can do that," said Mowgli. And he started to howl.

"One of the prettiest wild dogs is the fox," continued Mother Wolf. "It has a beautiful, bushy tail. The fox is very clever. The mother fox hides her family in a den and hunts at night. Sometimes you see the baby foxes playing outside their den in the early evening."

"Just like we do," said Mowgli.

"Other dogs live with people," said Mother Wolf.

"People? Who wants to live with them?" Mowgli said, snuggling up to his brothers and sisters.

"Well, you see, Mowgli," answered Mother Wolf, "long ago, dogs and people learned to help each other. People trained dogs to help them to hunt, to pull sleds, and to herd cattle.

"Dogs help to guard people's houses. And people
have dogs to keep them company — they are friends.
You can see many, many different kinds of pet dogs."

The next day, Mowgli talked to Hathi, the elephant.

"We are one of the largest animals," said Hathi, proudly. "Look at my baby son. He was born only yesterday, but already he is bigger and stronger than you!

"All the elephants in the herd help take care of him.

"When he grows up, this baby elephant will have large tusks like mine. These big ivory tusks are useful for digging up roots and making water holes. Sometimes elephants use their tusks in battle. But mostly, we are peaceful animals.

"Look how cleverly we use our long trunks. The mother elephant comforts and guides her baby with her trunk. And there is another elephant taking a shower with his trunk to keep cool.

"We use our large ears to fan ourselves and drive off flies. We show our feelings, too, by using our ears. When an elephant is angry, its ears stand straight out and it squeals loudly."

"Next to elephants, hippopotamuses and rhinoceroses are the biggest animals," said Hathi.

Hippos love the water. They lie in it, with only ears, eyes, and nostrils showing. They dive down and walk on the river bottom. Sometimes the babies ride on the mother's back. Hippos live together in big groups. They all help to take care of the babies.

Rhinos look like some of the dinosaurs from long ago. A rhino has a scaly coat of armor and a huge horn on its nose. Sometimes a mother rhino gently prods her baby with her horn to make it move.

Giraffes are the tallest animals in the world. A full-grown giraffe may be about the height of three tall people.

Giraffes are so tall they feed on the topmost branches of the tallest trees. They can see over the heads of smaller animals. They are the first to know when a hungry lion is near. When a giraffe runs away, all the other animals run, too.

"There are many other kinds of animals with hooves," said Hathi. "But of course, they are smaller than we mighty elephants. They all have long legs and can run fast."

Horses and their baby foals live with people. People like to ride on horseback, and sometimes use horses to pull wagons or plows.

The water buffalo has huge, curved horns. It is about the size of a small car and can be dangerous if it gets angry.

It stays near the water and likes to bathe in the mud. The calf feeds on its mother's milk. And sometimes it says, "Moo!" just like a farmyard calf.

Zebras are like small, fat horses with black-and-white-striped coats. Their babies learn to run with their mothers soon after they are born. Zebras live together and travel together. When there are many animals together it is difficult for hunters to catch any one of them.

Springboks, too, move around together. When it is surprised by something, the springbok springs in the air, twisting and turning!

The baby deer is called a fawn. It can stand and walk almost as soon as it is born. But for a few days the mother may move her fawn from one hiding place to another. She stays nearby, and comes back to feed her baby.

The baby's spotted coat is hard to see in the sun and the shade of the bushes, if the baby stays still. When it is grown, the deer no longer has spots on its coat.

Moose are large animals with huge, spreading antlers. The roar of a bull moose can be heard for miles through the forest.

Shaggy musk-oxen live near the North Pole. When there is danger, they huddle together in a furry circle, with their babies in the middle. Few animals are brave enough to attack the large bull musk-oxen, who stand on the outer ring of the circle. They are afraid of those slashing hooves and sharp horns!

Just then, Baloo the bear came lumbering by.

"What do you know of animals in cold countries?" sniffed Baloo to Hathi. "Come on, little Britches. I will tell you all about bears. We live everywhere—in steamy jungles and mountain dens and the icy cold of the north.

"We can stand up on two feet, just like you.

"And we like to play wrestling games, and roll over on our backs, and wave our paws!"

Bear cubs are born in hidden dens in the winter, when the mother is half asleep. She and the babies snooze until the days get longer and warmer.

Bear cubs are tiny at first. But they grow fast.

They learn to climb up trees or hide in their den when there is danger.

They learn to eat berries and fruit and honey. They catch fish. And some kinds of bears eat other animals.

The biggest bear of all is the polar bear. It grows to about 11 feet tall—that's taller than the tallest human!

Polar bears live in the ice of the far, far north, with their snowy white cubs.

"Some animals look like bears but really aren't bears," continued Baloo. "A panda is often called a bear, but it is really a relation of the raccoon. A panda is black and white and round and cuddly."

Pandas live high in the cool mountains of China. Not many people have seen pandas, except in zoos.

When panda babies are born they are even tinier than bear cubs. They weigh no more than mice. The big panda mother holds the baby in her arms. She feeds it and plays with it until it can take care of itself.

"The koala looks like a bear, but it is certainly not a bear," said Baloo. "It is a relative of the kangaroo.

"It has very thick gray hair. It has black-button eyes and a flat black nose.

"The koala eats so many eucalyptus leaves that people say it smells like a cough drop!"

"Not a bit like a bear," said Mowgli.

When a koala baby is born, it is no longer than a thumbnail. The baby crawls into its mother's pouch. And there it stays, until it is strong enough to crawl out and hang onto tree branches—or its mother's back.

A baby kangaroo, too, lives in its mother's pouch until it can jump around on its strong legs.

Suddenly Mowgli was swung into the air by a crowd of noisy monkeys. Chattering, they carried him from tree to tree. Mowgli felt as if he were flying through the air, but he was not afraid.

When the mischievous monkeys set him down, they all started talking at once.

"See how fast we can travel!"

"Look what long, strong arms and legs we have!"

"We have four fingers and a thumb, just as you do, Mowgli!"

"And we have them on our feet as well!"

"And with our long, wonderful tails we can hang upside down on branches if we want to!"

"See how tightly a baby monkey holds onto its mother's fur as she flies through the branches!"

"Monkeys are very, very clever," said Mowgli.

"Of course," said one of the monkeys when the chattering had died down, "there are apes, too."

"What are apes?" asked Mowgli.

The old monkey looked closely at the man-cub.

"They are a little like us . . . and a little like you," he said.

"Some of them are huge and have no tails," shrieked the other monkeys, giggling.

"But they are very clever," said the old monkey. "Gorillas are the largest. They can be as tall as men — and many times stronger. But they are peaceful animals. They take good care of all the babies in the family.

"Other apes, the chimpanzees and the orange-haired orangutans, care well for their babies, too. The babies cling to the long hair on their mothers' chests, or ride on the mothers' backs."

Suddenly the monkeys squealed and disappeared. Mowgli looked around to see what had frightened them away.

"Noisy chatterboxes."

It was Bagheera, the black panther. Bagheera had crept up behind Mowgli on his large, padded paws. His coat was shining and sleek, his whiskers long, and his big teeth white and as sharp as knives.

"Aw, Bagheera, did you have to scare them away?" Mowgli complained.

"Monkeys aren't my sort," replied Bagheera. "Let me tell you about a more noble family of animals—cats. All cats are beautiful, even our old enemy Shere Khan, the tiger. A tiger is also a cat—one of the biggest of our beautiful family."

A tiger's coat is gold and orange and white, striped with black. Tiger kittens are tiny when they are born. The tiger mother stays close, feeding them and fiercely driving away enemies. She carries her cubs in her mouth to move them to safety.

"And there are many other beautiful cats," said Bagheera. The lynx has soft, thick fur to keep it warm in the snow. It has tufted ears and snowshoe paws, and hardly any tail at all.

The jaguar has a wonderfully spotted coat. Like many cats, the jaguar and her cubs like to cool off and swim in the water.

The cougar, or puma, can leap up onto a rock high above it to escape its enemies!

Perhaps the greatest hunter of us all is the cheetah. It can run much faster than a horse. The little ones cannot keep up with the mother at first, but they soon learn.

"Most cats live alone and hunt alone, after their cubs have grown," said Bagheera. "But lions—lions are different."

"How so?" asked Mowgli.

"Lions live together in families called prides. The father lion is sometimes called the King of the Beasts. He wears a mane of heavy fur around his head and neck. His mighty roar can be heard for miles. But if you ask me," sniffed Bagheera, "he is a lazy fellow.

"The lionesses, the female lions, do most of the hunting. They look after each other's cubs. The cubs play just like all kittens. But each playtime is a time of learning, too. Cubs learn to hide and pounce. They stalk each other and make sudden dashes at each other. They watch the grown-ups, and soon they learn to do their share of the hunting.

"But it is always the 'king' of the pride who gets the first share of the meal—for that is the way of lions."

"And then, of course, there are the cats that live with people," said Bagheera.

"Really!" said Mowgli. "You mean that people own cats?"

"Oh, no," said Bagheera. "Nobody *owns* a cat. Cats decide to live with people. They let the people pet them and feed them and give them soft places to sleep. And in return the cats *purr* and look beautiful and make people happy.

"Many are dark and sleek, like me. Some are white."

Some house cats have thick, fluffy coats.

Some cats are striped.

Some have patches of black and white and orange.

Others, like the blue-eyed Siamese, have strange, loud voices.

And though house cats are fed good food, many of them still act like mighty hunters of the wild. They crouch and pounce and carry home rats and mice and other small animals.

"Rats and mice make very good food for cats," said Bagheera. "Rats and mice often live where people live. They eat people's food and chew their furniture."

But there are lots of chewing animals that live in the wild and do no harm.

The groundhog chews all summer and sleeps all winter. It digs underground tunnels in many places, so it can shelter in whatever hole is nearest.

This squirrel has a long, fluffy tail. When it finds a tasty nut, the squirrel may stuff it in its cheek pouch to eat later, or to hide underground.

The chipmunk scampers over the ground and up and down trees. Or it may sit up on its hind legs, staring around with its large eyes or twitching its nose.

When baby cottontail rabbits are born, they stay in a little den lined with their mother's soft fur until they are old enough to run and nibble on grass.

"Oh, a fur-lined bed sounds so cozy," said Mowgli.

Here is a mother skunk, with her string of little black-and-white babies. All animals are careful to stay away from the skunk. If this skunk gets scared by a porcupine, she will spray with a special liquid from beneath her tail. The spray smells very bad—and it may sting the porcupine's eyes.

Up in a tree a sleepy opossum carries her babies on her back to keep them safe. She is waiting for evening, when she will go hunting for eggs and fruit.

Down by the stream, a shiny-eyed raccoon is fishing. The little raccoon is furry and pretty. She is also very clever with her long fingers. She can catch fish, peel fruit, dig holes, and climb trees.

The raccoon babies are safe in their home in a hollow tree trunk.

Most animals don't have real "homes." They must keep moving to find food. But some, like beavers, live in family "homes" for a long time.

Beavers have long, sharp, yellow teeth. They chew and chew on a young tree until the tree falls down. Then they roll the tree down the bank of a river. Lots and lots of trees piled together make a dam, which is a kind of wall. The dam holds back the water of the stream. Soon there is a deep pond.

In the pond the beavers start to make their home, or "lodge." The lodge has different rooms. There is even a nursery for their babies. The beavers make "chimneys" so they can breathe when the pond is frozen over with ice.

Baby beavers help by chewing up twigs and leaves to fill in holes in the dam.

When the lodge gets too crowded, young beavers swim away to build homes of their own.

"It's nice to have a home," said Mowgli, yawning. "I think it's time for me to go home. Good-bye, Bagheera, and thanks." Mowgli started back to Mother Wolf's den.

"Welcome home, little Mowgli," said Mother Wolf.
"Nighttime is sleeping time for little Mowglis. All young
creatures must sleep and rest to become strong."

A baby monkey rests in its mother's arms.

Three spotted lion cubs curl up together.

Baby rabbits cuddle up in their burrow.

The raccoon babies are warm and sleepy now.

And little Mowglis, like all human children, say,
"Good night, sleep tight."